DANEL
CAVALCANTE BOOK

The Untold Truth Behind the murderer that killed

His Girlfriend, a Man in Brazil and Breaks out of

Chester Prison

JAMES A. GILSON

Copyright page

1

Table of contents

Introduction

I vividly recall the day I first heard about the Danelo Cavalcante murder case. It was a dismal, cloudy morning, and I was sipping on my coffee, going through the headlines on my laptop. As the news raced over the television, I couldn't help but be lured into the brewing horror that would soon grab our tiny town.

The tale seemed like something out of a criminal thriller. Danelo Cavalcante, a known killer, had been arrested for a brutal murder that sent shockwaves through our close-knit town. The deceased, a popular local business owner, had been brutally killed in a heist gone bad. The whole town was in grief, and a tangible dread hovered in the air.

As I went through the circumstances of the case, I couldn't help but feel a sensation of discomfort sinking into the pit of my stomach. The notion that such a cruel monster had been living amongst us all this time sent chills down my spine. I, like everyone else, watched the case intently as it made its way through the courts.

But then, just when we believed the horror was finished, a twist in the narrative left us all flabbergasted. Danelo Cavalcante had somehow managed to arrange a daring jail escape from Chester jail, the maximum-security institution where he was being kept. It was the type of narrative you'd expect to see in a Hollywood movie, not in our quiet village.

The days that followed were a haze of tension and terror. News of his escape dominated every discourse. We secured our doors, feared wandering alone at night, and even questioned the safety of our community. It seemed like our sense of security had been blown into a million pieces, and I couldn't escape the idea that danger lurked around every turn.

The search that followed was nothing short of epic. Helicopters soared above, police vehicles patrolled the streets, and sirens boomed through the night. The whole village held its breath, hoping for Danelo's arrest. It was as if we were living in a real-life thriller, and I couldn't help but worry how all of this would end.

Thirteen days seemed like an eternity as we eagerly waited for any word of Danelo's location. The tension in the air was tangible, and I couldn't avoid the impression that he was lurking in the shadows, watching our every move. The notion of a brutal killer on the loose tormented my thoughts, and I found it impossible to concentrate on anything else.

Then, one fateful evening, the news we had all been waiting for finally arrived. Danelo Cavalcante had been caught. It was a communal sigh of relief that flowed across our community. The search had concluded, and justice would be served.

As I watched the news of his arrest spread on my TV, I couldn't help but dwell on the rollercoaster of emotions I had experienced during this journey. From shock and dread to optimism and relief, it had been a traumatic trip for all of us. Our community had gone through the unspeakable, and yet, we had emerged stronger and more unified than ever before.

The Danelo Cavalcante murder case and his audacious jail escape had left an indelible impact on our tiny community, a warning that even in the most serene settings, evil might find its way in. But as we went on, I couldn't help but feel that we had also regained the power and tenacity that linked our community together. We had conquered our darkest fears and emerged triumphant, ready to tackle whatever difficulties lay ahead, together.

In the days after Danelo Cavalcante's arrest, our community started to slowly recover to a semblance of normality. The continuous police presence started to lessen, and the stress that had seized our town for weeks began to relax. It felt as if a weight had been lifted off our shoulders, and we could finally breathe again.

The apprehension of Danelo was a monument to the relentless efforts of law enforcement, the unflinching resolve of our town, and the strength of a community together in the face of tragedy. It was a reminder that justice may triumph, even in the darkest of times.

The narrative of Danelo Cavalcante's murder case and his daring jail escape would long be imprinted in our memory, a reminder of the courage that could be found in the face of hardship and the power of a community united in pursuit of justice. It was a narrative of tenacity, optimism, and the unyielding spirit of a little community that refused to be defined by sorrow.

CHAPTER 1

Biography of Danelo Cavalcante

Danelo Cavalcante, a Brazilian national, has been the target of a huge search in Pennsylvania, barely one week after receiving a life sentence for a heinous murder. His life took a dark turn, earning him fame on both sides of the Atlantic.

Cavalcante's life took a catastrophic and violent turn in Brazil, leading him down a road of crime and devastation. He did a horrific deed in April 2021 that would permanently affect the lives of all involved. He stabbed his ex-girlfriend, Deborah Brandao, to death in front of her two young children, who were four and seven years old at the time. During the terrible and heinous act, Brandao received 38 stab wounds.

Cavalcante was apprehended quickly, but his journey into darkness did not stop there. He had an open murder warrant in Brazil for a prior offense, showcasing his violent record even more. In 2017, he was suspected of murdering a guy in his own country who owed him money.

Cavalcante was caught in Virginia after the murder of Brandao, which led to his prosecution in Pennsylvania. The result was a life sentence, guaranteeing that he would never have the chance to hurt innocent people again. But destiny had other intentions.

Cavalcante managed to escape from Chester County jail in West Chester, Pennsylvania, barely one week after being condemned to life in jail. The specifics of his escape are unknown since prison authorities have been tight-lipped about the event, only saying that an inquiry is ongoing.

Cavalcante's escape sparked a regional search involving dozens of law enforcement organizations. Residents within a six-mile radius of the facility have been notified of the situation and advised to use utmost care. In their attempts to find him, officials have used a variety of tools, including dogs, drones, and helicopters.

Cavalcante's dangerous position is not restricted to the United States; he is also sought for murder in Brazil, heightening the urgency of his arrest. Officials are advising the public not to approach him under any circumstances and to call 911 immediately if they have any information about his location.

The escape shook the neighborhood, causing West Chester University, which is situated near the jail, to temporarily postpone courses as a preventative measure.

The US Marshals Service and local officials have offered a $10,000 (£7,889) reward for information leading to the arrest of Danelo Cavalcante, a man who has gone from being a convicted killer to a wanted fugitive. His entire tale is a disturbing reminder of human nature's lowest depths and the importance of justice in the face of such horrible atrocities.

CHAPTER 2

Pennsylvania crime history

Cavalcante was convicted in the United States of murdering his ex-girlfriend, Deborah Brandao, in front of her children in 2021. Prosecutors claim he sought to prevent her from informing authorities about his involvement in the Brazil homicide.

Cavalcante was arrested in April 2021 after stabbing Brandao more than a dozen times in the chest and upper body in front of her 7-year-old daughter and 3-year-old son, according to prior reports.

Brandao died later that day in the hospital after her daughter rushed to a neighbor's home and called 911.

Cavalcante was apprehended in Virginia while attempting to escape to Mexico and then back to Brazil.

On August 16, Cavalcante was found guilty of first-degree murder and condemned to life in jail without the possibility of release. In Brazil, he is still wanted for a murder committed in 2017.

How Danelo Cavalcante was apprehended

Danelo Cavalcante, an escaped killer, was apprehended Wednesday morning after officials tracked him down using thermal heat technology from an airplane before a U.S. Border Patrol tactical unit dog eventually pinned him down, according to authorities.

Cavalcante, a 34-year-old convicted murderer who escaped from jail on Aug. 31, was apprehended wearing a Philadelphia Eagles sweatshirt after almost two weeks on the run.

He was taken in a convoy to the Avondale State Police barracks, where he arrived covered in a foil blanket soon before 9 a.m., according to Pennsylvania State Police Lt. Col. George Bivens.

Except for a small dog bite, Cavalcante stated he had no severe injuries.

In a public radio transmission at 8:18 a.m., Chester County officials were heard reporting Cavalcante's arrest.

The Chester County administration, the radio room, and several other organizations are all collaborating on the prisoner's escape. The culprit has been caught, I'm happy to say. "The subject is in custody," stated a Chester County officer.

Police gave 24-hour security to his victim's family, and police vehicles played recordings of Cavalcante's mother pleading with him to surrender in Portuguese.

The arrest came a day after police in northern Chester County established an 8- to 10-square-mile perimeter.

Bivens said that a burglar alarm went off soon after midnight at a property inside the perimeter, which was examined but no sign of Cavalcante was found.

Around 1 a.m. Wednesday, a Drug Enforcement Administration aircraft picked up a heat signal and began tracking it, and tactical teams descended on the area.

According to Bivens, a lightning storm led the aircraft to depart the region and temporarily hindered the tracking procedure. According to him, tactical forces seized the location and held it overnight until the aircraft could return.

Tactical teams concentrated on the heat source in a forested location west of PA 100 just after 8 a.m. on Wednesday.

The teams had "the element of surprise," according to Bivens.

He said that until that moment, Cavalcante was unaware that he was being encircled. "He began to crawl through thick underbrush, taking his rifle with him," Bivens stated, adding that Cavalcante still had a 22-caliber weapon that he had taken the night before.

The Border Patrol Tactical Unit was on the scene with a dog that eventually subdued Cavalcante, and team members from BORTAC and Pennsylvania State Police stepped in.

"He resisted arrest, but he was taken into custody, and no one was injured," Bivens added.

He said that the surprise assault and the employment of the Border Patrol dog had a "large role" in stopping Cavalcante from deploying the pistol.

Cavalcante was transferred to the Avondale station for additional processing and questioned after medical authorities examined the bite. He will eventually be transferred to a state jail facility to complete the remainder of his life term.

It gives me great pleasure to be present here this morning and speak with everyone of you about concluding this manhunt effectively and, above all, without hurting anybody else, said Bivens.

When questioned why cops photographed Cavalcante after his arrest, Bivens stated he was aware of the picture opportunity.

"Those people put in a tremendous amount of effort in the face of hardship." They feel good about the work they did. "I'm not bothered at all that they took a photo of him in custody," he stated. "I appreciate their efforts and wish them luck,"

The multi-agency search for Cavalcante, 34, drew national attention for over two weeks. Officials were compelled to constantly broaden their search radius after the murder prisoner snuck through it.

During the 14-day experience, Cavalcante survived by eating watermelons stolen from a farm. He also took a vehicle and a .22 rifle and has recently admitted to planning a carjacking and fleeing to Canada.

Cavalcante was charged with fresh crimes related to his jailbreak only hours after his capture. He is already spending life in jail for the violent death of his former ex-girlfriend Deborah Brandao, 33, in April 2021.

Brazilian prosecutors are now planning to charge Cavalcante in connection with a 2017 murder in which the murder prisoner is implicated.

CHAPTER 3

A chronology of the hunt for the escaped Pennsylvania murderer

Surveillance cameras in the search area had seen the fleeing murderer many times. Images of the escapee reveal that he was able to shave and change clothing during his stay on the outside.

On August 16, 2023, he was convicted of first-degree murder and criminal possession in the death of Brando.

He was sentenced to life in prison without the chance of release on August 22, 2023.

He escaped from the Chester County Prison in West Chester, Pennsylvania, on August 31, 2023.

On September 2, 2023, at about 12:30 a.m., he was observed on a house security video in the 1800 block of Lenape Road, about a mile and a half from the Chester County Prison.

On September 3, 2023, a Pennsylvania State Police trooper noticed him from a distance and pursued him, but owing to the terrain and other hurdles, the officer was unable to apprehend the fugitive.

He was seen by a trail camera at Longwood Gardens in Kennett Square, Pennsylvania, on September 4, 2023, while he was traveling north at 8:21 p.m. and returning south at 9:33 p.m.

He was discovered on Chandler Road in Pennsbury Township, Pennsylvania, on September 5, 2023.

He stole a 2020 Ford Transit van from Baily's Dairy Farm in West Chester on September 9, 2023, but abandoned it in a field behind a barn farther west in East Nantmeal Township, Pennsylvania when it ran out of petrol.

A vehicle saw a guy hunkered in the timberline along the south side of Fairview Road west of Route 100, and response teams subsequently discovered his jail shoes.

On the same night, a homeowner claimed to have shot fire on Cavalcante after seeing him taking a gun in the garage. According to police, the detainee was not injured in the incident.

On September 10, 2023, he was photographed in Phoenixville, Pennsylvania, with a new look. That day, Pennsylvania State Police Lieutenant Colonel George Bivens verified that his sister Eleni had been detained by US Immigration and Customs Enforcement for immigration violations.

On September 11, 2023, at about 10:00 p.m., he broke into the garage of a house on Coventryville Road in Pottstown, Pennsylvania, and took a 22 rifle. As he ran with the firearm, the homeowner fired at him.

On September 13, 2023, just after 8:00 a.m., he was apprehended in a forested region of West Chester County.

The on-duty guard

A massive search was begun when security video showed the 5-foot-2, 120-pound Cavalcante crab walking up a set of parallel walls onto the top of Chester County Prison in Pocopson Township on Aug. 31.

A county spokeswoman said that an 18-year veteran guard who failed to notice Cavalcante's escape was sacked. According to the county official, the guard, who has not been named, was using a smartphone in the tower, which is against Chester County Prison regulations.

CHAPTER 4

Cavalcante: what people say

Calvacante was observed being brought to the state police facility to jail at 2 p.m. Wednesday.

Cavalcante was handcuffed and treated for a dog bite he received while being apprehended. Cavalcante was stripped of his attire — black prison trousers and a stolen Eagles sweatshirt that Governor Josh Shapiro has since vowed to replace for the rightful owner — and brought in a tactical unit van to the state police's Avondale barracks.

The procedure took four hours. Cavalcante was "brutally honest" about his two weeks of escaping arrest in an interview with law enforcement and a Portuguese translator, according to Supervisory Deputy US Marshall Robert Clark.

Cavalcante will be brought to a state correctional institution where "he will be housed for the foreseeable future," according to Pennsylvania Attorney General Michelle Henry, but it is unclear which facility. The jail, which formerly imprisoned Bill Cosby, was erected in 2018 and is a maximum-security institution with a prisoner-to-staff ratio of 3.2 to 1.

He was arraigned on Wednesday on a felony escape charge filed on August 31.

Prosecutors requested that Cavalcante be held in custody during his arraignment since he had already been sentenced to life in prison, according to Henry. Cavalcante was refused bail by Magisterial District Judge Michael Iacocca.

According to the charge papers, he is scheduled to appear in court again on September 27 for a preliminary hearing. More charges might be made against Cavalcante for the thefts he committed during his escape, as well as many house invasions in the vicinity that have yet to be shown to be related to the felon.

Sarah Brando, the murder victim's sister, expressed thanks for the help her family got throughout the search.

On Wednesday, she posted on social media that her family is "processing everything that has happened while taking care of ourselves."

The last two weeks, she added, "have been really traumatic and terrible because they've brought back all the memories of losing my sister and the fear that the offender could harm us again. So that we may collect ourselves and find out how to get through this sad event, I humbly ask that our privacy be honored.

Chester County commissioners stated in a statement Wednesday that Cavalcante's arrest "ends the nightmare of the past two weeks," and they praised the numerous law enforcement agencies that worked together to catch him.

Marian Moskowitz, Josh Maxwell, and Michelle Kichline, the commissioners, stated that the county's prison officials have made "some immediate changes to bolster security," have hired security contractors to make permanent changes to exercise yards, and are reviewing changing procedures for security measures and communication with residents who live near prison grounds.

Statement by Cavalcante

Cavalcante said that he ate stolen farm melons, drank water from a brook, and hid behind deep thickets where he could stay concealed from sight until someone walked on him. He'd put his feces behind leaves to obscure his footprints.

The fugitive acknowledged having multiple near encounters with search forces.

Cavalcante was led out of the barracks wearing a medical gown when the procedure was completed.

He had chains on his feet and was barefoot.

In in the meantime, Tocantins state prosecutors have accused Cavalcante of "dual qualified homicide" in the 2017 killing of Válter Jurior Moreira dos Reis in Figueirópolis. They claim this was because of a debt the victim allegedly owed him for auto upkeep.

Prosecutors want to begin a trial next month, according to the Brazilian news publication Folha de Sao Paulo. Dayane Moreira dos Reis, Moreira dos Reis' sister, told the magazine that she felt Cavalcante's escape encouraged prosecutors to reconsider the case.

"Justice moves at a glacial pace." She told Folha de Sao Paulo that they had waited 7 years for a response. It didn't help that my brother even promised to pay for the repairs before he passed away and told him not to worry.

Due to his continuing legal proceedings in America, the prosecutor's office allegedly pushed against Cavalcante being added to Interpol's wanted list. According to Folha de Sao Paulo, Brazilian officials say they have begun conversations with the US Embassy in an attempt to move the process along.

CHAPTER 5

Danelo Cavalcante's mother justifies killings

The mother of a convicted killer who was apprehended Wednesday after almost two weeks on the run has justified her son's actions, claiming he "had no other choice" than to kill his ex-girlfriend.

In an interview on Tuesday, Danelo Cavalcante's mother, Iracema, blamed his girlfriend, Deborah Brandao, for her death.

"Did it happen? It occurred. But it occurred because of the squeeze she placed on him, the posture she took with him," Iracema said of her son stabbing Brandao to death while her small son and daughter were there.

Iracema said that there was no femicide. "He had no choice but to."

In that situation, Iracema alleges, Valtar Jnior Moreira dos Reis threatened to murder her son first.

She is now concerned about what will happen to her kid, who was spotted being led into a vehicle by a SWAT squad on Wednesday.

But Iracema told the Times that she now worries for Danelo, believing that life in jail or death at the hands of the police would be unfair.

"If I said my son didn't make a mistake, I'd be lying," she added.

"I know what my kid did was bad. I know my kid should pay for his error. But I want my kid to pay for his error with dignity, not with his life."

She went on to explain that if Danelo faced life in a maximum-security prison, he could be better off dying.

"If [the choice is] to go to a place to suffer and die in that place, it's better to die soon," she remarked. You are not required to go over all of this simply to pass away later.

"Today, I see my son as dead in a strange place, trampled, and everyone just lying about him, saying he's something he's not," Iracema continued.

Truth about the dog that assisted in the capture of Danelo Cavalcante

A US Border Patrol spokeswoman stated that the 4-year-old Belgian Malinois shepherd assisted in the detention of Danelo Cavalcante in South Coventry Township on Wednesday morning.

"Border Patrol agents and [Yoda] surprised Cavalcante, who surrendered without firing his weapon," according to a spokeswoman.

According to Deputy U.S. Marshal Robert Clark, the dog bit Cavalcante's scalp before latching onto his leg, "at which time Cavalcante submitted."

"I think he was in a lot of pain at that point," Clark added. "He was probably in excruciating pain."

At a press conference on Wednesday, State Police Lt. Col. George Bivens said that police dogs serve a "very important role" in securely subduing people. Law enforcement canines are taught to attack just once and then release on command.

Yoda is a member of an El Paso, Texas-based tactical squad. The Belgian Malinois is a "smart, confident, and versatile" breed that works hard and creates unbreakable ties with people, according to the American Kennel Club.

Belgian Malinois, which are smaller and lighter than German Shepherds, are commonly sought after by law enforcement organizations for K-9 operations.

The breed has aided handlers in a range of settings, from US military operations in Afghanistan to White House secret service assignments.

Conclusion

The terrible narrative of Danelo Cavalcante, a name that became associated with violence and escape, serves as a striking reminder of the complexity and evil that can pervade the human experience. His life's journey, defined by violence, escape, and worldwide repercussions, compels us to ponder on the depths of human nature, the quest for justice, and the tenacity of the human spirit.

Cavalcante's arrest after the murder of Deborah Brandao should have marked the end of his reign of evil. However, it was learned that he had an outstanding murder warrant in Brazil, adding another dimension to his violent background. The trial in Pennsylvania resulted in a life sentence, presumably ensuring that he would never damage innocent lives again. But destiny had other intentions.

Printed in Great Britain
by Amazon

32264594R00020